The Horizon Shifts Sideways

The Horizon Shifts Sideways

Alison Thompson

PUNCHER & WATTMANN

First published in 2024
Published by Puncher & Wattmann
PO Box 279
Waratah NSW 2298

info@puncherandwattmann.com

NATIONAL
LIBRARY
OF AUSTRALIA

A catologue record for this book is available from The National Library of Australia.

ISBN   9781922571922

Cover photograph: Matthew Cheli
Cover design by Miranda Douglas
Printed by Lightning Source International

Contents

For Tim and Carrie

The Sound of Red

– on seeing our neighbour slaughter the Jersey calf

My mind refuses this memory.
I think instead of red, of a dress I once owned, of walking
the streets of Naples, of tomatoes and chillies in a summer garden,
of a teenage brother accelerating out the drive
of my daughter slamming the door – a beyond-words slam.

It is the sound of embers, of fire-talk, of distant caverns,
ancient times. I can feel these things, remember them; though
            they're things
I can't know, things etched deep into ancestor memory, hard –
wired in my brain. The thud
of tides and rockfalls; the pulse of air through forests and plains.

But blood returns. Blood like red like a history I can't read.
This is the blood that swells the heart's cave: magenta, crimson.

I was the oldest child. I thought I knew what death was.
When he took the blade to the calf's throat I didn't breathe.
His daughter, younger than me, held my hand.
As soon as I could, I let go.

Flying Fox

Like seals on land
they are awkward out of their natural element.
They claw across wet grass,
ply avocadoes to the ground,
strip the skin from lemons and lime.

This night-time raid is disturbed by the dog:
they scramble like fighter pilots,
wheeling into the sky at the barked alarm.

Next morning, my feet squelch
on the warm mess of their destruction
while they are elsewhere, slung safely
upside down,
crowding night-raiders hypnotised by dawn.

Amphibious

After months of dry weather garlands of rain
fill the empty dam – six inches in a single night –

as I lie semi-awake, my insomniac brain gauging each drop,
measuring each wave and surge in the fan-resistant heat.

Thoughts swell in my consciousness like poisonous toads
emerging from mud-sleep – their shrill croaking set on repeat.

At dawn the rain ceases and the mind-toads retreat.
I swim free of my bedclothes, breathe air. Daybreak,

with its piss-weak sun, brings with it a watery kind of hope
and I get up, shower and dress, call myself an optimist.

Cocoon

For eight years your body lay on the floor of your Sydney
house, a three-storey terrace overlooking Centennial Park,
the drawn curtains
shutting out the view.

All they found were folded bones
eased down between a table and chair,
indistinguishable at first
from the patterned swirls of the carpet.

Now strangers mark your passing in newspapers and poems.
In the slums of the world,
no-one dying takes this long to be found.
I like to think when they opened that room your soul flew.

Legacy

Extinct

These birds have only parchment wings now
      deft and delicate strokes painted by a man
with an eye for detail   a precise individual
      delighting in minutiae

a man who marvels at the complexity of each feather
      the fragile shivery quality of each separate barb
at how the tiny iridescent shards of colour   stitch in the light
      and make the whole wing shine

How gravely he holds the still warm corpse
      turning it from hand to hand, extending each wing
examining the underside   the belly
      the curled feet, the flaccid neck

How gently he places it on the bench
      to tag, weigh, measure   recording
each detail   in his leather-bound book
      before he turns aside

with an emotion he might, if pressed, have called *reverence*
      and sets to work with pen and brush
omitting   the smudge of crimson
      on the pale breast feathers

omitting the fall of the bird to the ground
      that very morning
when Thomas   (his shooter)
      had dropped it with a single shot

Pest

This morning it all seems very English in my garden
what with the overcast sky, the chickens
on the back lawn and the fox   who stared straight through the window
as I rose half-asleep   to see what had set the chickens off

And I, *colonial* to my bones, forgot he was vermin
feral, noxious   fated to be culled
forgot he was anything other   than a villain of fairytales
and held my dog's collar   as I held his gaze

He stood assured, not even hungry,
just checking things out, never doubting his right to belong –
to take what is offered to him   willing to adapt
Remembering the chickens   I let the dog go

but the fox was long gone, loping lazily
up the hill to his home among eucalypt and lantana
yet another new arrival   that has made its place here
without asking   without shame

And of the three of us   fox, lantana, European
I wonder who least understands this land
who has rendered   the most harm
who most deserves   the poison

Indigo Valley Eulogy

Two decades on I have found a way
to be grateful for your death: not its fact, rather
the ease of its coming – a usual day delivering the mail –
the valley unfolding before you, causing you to pause now and again
when a view surprised you into noting the spot as a good place to sketch.
Even the exact moment I can think of with wonder, the whirring
of the car engine against Stievans' mailbox,
the bus driver stepping down from the school bus
on the return run to find you resting against the steering wheel,
already dreaming your next painting into eternity.

Perhaps you knew – gulping down two angina tablets before setting out
and taking the packet with you. I suppose you should have called
your doctor but having witnessed the hospital formalities
of other deaths, who would deny you that bright
untrammeled day – that final landscape
to immerse yourself in, and I
to remember you by.

Geebung, near Braidwood

This is barefoot country
even now, in early winter
when the cool mountain air dampens
the risk of a startled snake rising
in your path.

This is sitting-still country —
where the bracken unfurls its fronds
and where the layered view of the purple hills
makes you contemplate your place
in the natural order of things.

This is cracking bark country
where a distant haze of smoke drives
a shudder through the core of the old growth trees —
that yearn and lean toward
the merest hint of flame.

This is vast night country,
a curving roof of blackness shot through with stars —
points of light reaching across time —
and you wonder at the significance
of a self-aggrandising world.

This is stony swamp country —
as springy as the moss on the southside of the trees —
as pitted and tender as the bruise you find
on the sole of your foot three days
after you return home.

Flare

When she touched him on the arm late in the afternoon,
around the time the guests were spilling out of the house
to walk barefoot on the lawn,
his skin flared
as if caught in a grassfire.

Later he remembered the sounds that filtered in –
the laughter of guests, his wife's voice
in the kitchen,
the chained-up dogs,
children running on gravel.

In that whispered corner where he held back
from kissing her they stood together, his lips
brushing the hair at the side of her head,
naked, burning,
invisible to the world.

Trading armadillos

By fifty he'd traded it all: the car, the wife, the house,
    the only thing left to be rid of
        was his heart.

In the park a woman said, I'll trade you an armadillo, so
        they swapped, and he settled the armadillo deep within his chest
           where it fitted neatly, seemed the right weight.

He felt pride in its vigor, rejoiced
    at the new strength lying within him but soon
        he became restless, he began to feel endangered,
           found himself suffocating. As the pain in his chest rose
               he wondered how his heart had survived in the outside world?
            Had it formed a protective shell – or a tongue to eat worms?
        And as the armadillo clawed its way free the dying man
    looked up and saw that his heart had sprouted wings
and was perched in a tree, tremulously beating,
    singing its freedom softly
        like a cautious bird.

Four Poems of Love

What do you know?

Not secrets but knowledge
like the sound of your son thunking down the stairs
the sound of finches under the carport scuttling at your arrival
the change in your daughter's voice
when she's tired   the colour of your lover's eyes
as they look past you out the window

What things inhabit your heart?

Bloodwoods; and sap dripping down the side of a young black wattle
the stickiness of it on your fingers   your mother
fumbling at the catheter in her arm   the face of your father
in death   an awareness of the angle at which a kestrel
hovers over the grass on the road to your house

What do you remember?

checking rabbit traps with your brother in the early morning
hearing your father swear in the shed   down the back
your mother's laugh as he swirled her around the room
the scent of kauri pine   as you open the cutlery drawer
of the kitchen hutch   in your grandmother's house

What have you lost?

the comfort of talking to parents on the phone   the inclination
to learn an instrument   the desire to run fast and jump
the face of youth and the yearning to swim in cold water
the notion of how things should be   in this world
the desire   to live forever

Radiance

He stops her in the supermarket to say he's found God   pitching too close
in his eagerness while she stares at his thinning hair   the slight paunch
struggles to remember the lithe young man   naked in her sunlit flat
where they'd made love on an inflatable mattress remembers more easily
the searching   the tears
and the terrible anger   that came in waves

How his whole body shook that night   he'd trembled Christ-like
on the balcony denouncing himself   again and again
how she'd held his arms   refused to let go
all the while talking   in her calmest voice
until the police came   her flat mates behind her
murmuring a modern prayer   of hold on hold on hold on

She'd left him then of course   ceased to be his disciple
but as he presses the leaflet into her hands   she notices
whilst his palms are a little sweaty   his back a little bent
he still has the eyes of a broken saint   and as he turns to leave
she reaches out and touches him   smiles
as radiant as a supplicant   and says I'm glad

The Wounded Pelican

The noises he makes don't seen birdlike. Without a syrinx
he is limited to grunts and rumbles, hisses and barks.
He sulks in the cage's far corner, his back turned
on his captors. So far, he has refused all food,
averting his gaze when they crouch at the door
proffering fat fish and making cooing sounds
like those they might make to a kitten.
At last, in exasperation,
they skip the fish across the floor to his feet.
He flaps his good wing, shimmies his feathers,
lengthens his neck, then positions his bill underneath
his wing. No you don't, they say, and he shuffles
deep into the corner as they wrestle him down
and prise open his beak. The half-frozen fish
slides down his gullet then he heaves it back up
with a rush of sour seawater that douses their feet
Bloody Pelican.
As they leave, he grunts and huffs, turns
his back on them again. Later, as the moon
lights the bars of his cage, he clacks his beak
and flicks up the fish,
flipping and turning each one
until they point headfirst down his throat
on the swallow. As the moon sets, he lets his damaged wing
droop to the floor and sleeps. Next morning
he is docile, takes fish straight from their hands.
He tolerates being lifted, endures their manipulations
with eyes closed, his body tensed and rigid
against their alien clasp. The incongruity of hands
on feathers, the staccato snap of fingers on bill-skin,
needles like shards of fishbone lodged in his muscle.
The anonymity of anaesthetic rewiring his brain.
As he awakes, he stiffens against the weft and graft

of suture, the grip of tape and cloth,
the way it barbs his feathers, nips his skin.

Six weeks later he stands on the timber pier and blinks
in the pallor of the morning sky. He shakes,
not unlike a dog, tests his wings, easing them out full span,
remaining stock-still as the breeze fills the space underneath.
It appears, for a moment, as if he sighs,
then he leans to the wind, and his body
ripples and clicks into action – a rapid-fire waddle across the platform.
At the edge he turns back with a grunt and one last look –
the first from that yellow-bordered Oligocene eye
that meets their eyes – an ancient gaze that traverses
thirty-odd million years. After this there's no turning back.
As he hops down into the ribbon of water flowing fast
below the pier he lets loose a final guttural hiss and a bark
that reverberates across the inlet and all those strange
unfeathered creatures perched high above him
begin to whoop, whistle, and cheer.

Daughter, aged three

You come from bed
as if spilled from a snowstorm,
your face smooth and creased all at once,
your small body honey-warm
with sleep
and, opening each eye in turn, you
yawn as if you have all the time in the world
and nothing matters more
than waking up.

Horizons

The Boat

It's old, this boat. Rusting metal, blue and orange flakes of paint
peeling off into the water as the small boy watches, leaning out
over the edge, fascinated by the swirling trail of froth and foam
disappearing behind the stern.
He likes the clearness of this day, the first calm one since they left
and it fills his head like a sound, like a memory. With his head full
he can imagine running across hard ground again, imagine
an unwavering horizon.

The Small Boy and the Architect

who is his father and is taking him away, though heartbreak was involved.
How does one decide irrational things rationally?
They lost the others, and having lost them, all choices changed.
Perhaps they are on some other boat, are the words the architect speaks
against the breath of the wind and the boy –
who is more observant than most –
wonders why his father's lips are moving.

The Woman Who Has Lost her Children

is not a mother, but a teacher. She is finding out what is important.
It is not as she'd suspected: that she is alive.
She wishes she had stayed but what for? Her class had gone.
Everyone gone. She watches the small boy with longing,
notes the architect father's beard. Each half-hour
she retches over the edge – bile only.
It does not seem possible to eat.

The Prospect of Never Reaching Land

This is the collective thought – that something will happen.
To prevent their arrival somewhere. After all, much has already happened.
The small boy knows this – more has happened in the last month
than in his whole life. He is not even sure this other place exists.
He holds his father's hand, watches his lips move.
Don't pray, he thinks, don't pray –
all the gods are deaf.

The Captain Who Has Given Himself the Title

is happy to be on the boat, even a rusty old tankard like this.
It would be helpful to know where they are meant to be going, though.
He likes the look of the schoolteacher; she has firm thighs
and the sorrow in her eyes makes him, when he is drunk,
want to hold her and stroke her hair. The worst thing
about this apocalypse is he'll have to give up drinking.

The Others

are below deck. They still think they have something to lose, and fear
has them scrambling for cover. They speak a different language,
and when the woman tried to help them, they spat at her,
threw things at her, said words that echoed like curses.
Even the children would not look directly at her.
For a time, she remained there crouching, her hands helpless.
The self-styled captain knows their language, refuses to speak it.

The Dream of Somewhere Else

is the dream lost within all of us, an escape from danger
or boredom. In the West the architect was rich, in the East,
famous in a small-town kind of way. He eyes the boat
up and down its length, looks for angles, lines of perspective.
What house will they be able to build, he thinks?
What kind of house can you build on moving water, on memories that
  don't exist?

The Quiet Girl Who Thinks She's Hiding

The others, those above board, leave her alone. It's clear
she's been violated in some way. She thinks they can't see her
and they know, even the lousy drunkard of a captain, that it's better
she thinks this. Each day the small boy takes some food and pushes it
under the tarpaulin she sleeps under. Each day she eats it.
Never once does her mind ask where it comes from.
The desire for survival is a hungry mouse, strangely persistent.

The Horizon

seems like a movie they can't quite catch the plot of.
By now they are all fascinated. The others have come up on deck,
tired of their own fear. The small boy talks, not in words, but
in sounds that reach into the other children. They start to play.
The woman watches them, cries a little, eats a little.
The architect watches too, thinks they are too thin, thinks
they are not likely to survive.
He turns again to the shifting water, the ever-present greyness
of the ocean. He is counting the angles, estimating the arcs of waves.
Up on the higher deck, the captain is wishing for a drink
stronger than water, and for a desire stronger than drink.

He decides he will save the woman if he can, but is not sure
what he will really choose when it comes to it.
The small boy pauses in his game, points to something red floating
in the water. It is a small piece of plastic, an insignificant thing.
The children watch it as it disappears. The boy turns, sees
the quiet girl standing on the deck. He raises his hand.
She is standing near the other adults. She does not respond.
The horizon shifts again, sideways this time.

Drinking Rain

November in Sydney started with stinking rain,
minor floods and reports of cars getting stuck

having ploughed through deep water too fast.
Like me. During exams I'd sit drench-legged

and steam over the paper, my glasses fogged.
On the last night my rented room became the arena

for a waterfall as the ceiling collapsed
in an imperfect circle one bucket wide.

You wouldn't call it a leak, more like a rend
but when the rain stopped, I could see the stars

and I thought of you, out of the city
in that green leafy suburb

sipping your mother's soup,
protected from the rain.

The Man Who Trained Spiders

Had little trouble in general with insects
Cockroaches fetched the paper each morning
Ladybirds tended the garden & a team of ants
With military precision brought in the mail
Letter by letter to his feet

Bees brought him honey & hummed soothingly
Butterflies danced for his entertainment & grasshoppers
Kept his lawn down to a neat & tidy level
Of course, some were not worth the effort
The caterpillars too busy gorging, the wasps too busy killing

Only the arachnids bothered him
Sometimes obedient, sometimes not –
They looked at him with eight knowing eyes
Seeming to pause & consider, reserving the right
To choose their own actions

The man who trained spiders
Had trouble sleeping

The Evolution of Markus Long

The day Markus Long turned forty-five he woke early,
went downstairs into the clear still morning,
opened the garden shed and took out a spade.
He pulled on thick gloves and leather boots then
quietly closed the shed door.
He set off down the road along a fire-trail
leading into the forest until he came to a clearing
where a perfect diamond of sky could be seen above.
He began to dig.
The ground was loamy and soft and as he dug his breath
rose in misty pockets, mingling with the dank smell
of decaying leaves and the tang
of morning eucalyptus. After a while he paused.
The hole was shallow and wide, about three feet across
and a foot and a half deep.
He took off his boots and stepped into the centre.
He used the spade to drag the piled-up soil over his feet,
wriggling his toes so dirt trickled between them.
It felt moist, but oddly enough, not cold.
When the hole was filled, he tamped it down gently
with the spade then leaned to his left and propped the spade
against a sapling. He threw his gloves onto the ground
then stood up straight, arms held loosely out to each side.

He stood for a long time, all through that day and the next,
watching how the days came and went.
He felt a hard burst of heat as the sun reached its peak,
blasting down on his head. Just before dawn
he felt the cold seeping into each cell of his body
and wondered how long he could stand
the ache in his back,
in his limbs.

He was astonished when a small creature scurried up his body
and buried itself in his armpit, then spent an afternoon listening
to the tiny flutter of its heart
against his skin.

His thoughts jumped from one thing to the next, from
  the present
    to the future
      to the past.

He thought of his wife, tried to hold a picture of her
in his head but kept being interrupted by a glimpse
of something new in the forest.

It took him years to relax,
  decades to let go,
    centuries to begin
      to understand.

His thoughts became fractured, discontinuous.
Time no longer seemed linear.

He lost track of the number of arms and fingers he had.
When his toes started branching out into the soil he resisted,
feeling panic at being slowly sucked into the earth,
but eventually he began to feel strong, to feel
firmly planted.
He absorbed every sound and sensation,
the changes in the seasons, anticipated
when each tree would bloom, when the dollar-birds
would arrive and when the cicadas emerged.

Gradually he lost his fear of the unexpected,

the whine of a chainsaw,
         the lightning strikes,
                  the startling night-time noises.

When the fire came, roaring its echoless roar
through the forest he had been sure
he would be obliterated, but afterward he felt strangely calm,
sensing the new growth beginning to stir
beneath his singed hide. Old dead limbs crashed
to the forest floor and possums and gliders moved in.
His ears became hollows for small birds and when he tried
to open his eyes he found they had been eaten away by grubs.
His body expanded and grew until it towered
over everything
and his crown reached out into the sky.

Now the only thought he possessed was not a thought at all,
just a realisation beyond thought. He was the forest.

He opened his mouth to call out but his lips
had become whorls in the bark forming an 'O'
and his name was nothing more

than birds overhead, calling
      Maark,
           Maark,
                Maark.

In my Newsfeed

Images of Afghanistan, again.
Tonight, the evening sky is the world
hurled upside down.

Jesus in the Surf at Bondi

after Geoff Page, 'Christ at Gallipoli'

He's drawn the crowd, looking half-crazed as he hurls
himself into the surf; daring the rip on a winter's day.

The ocean tosses him back and for a moment he lies
on the sand gasping for breath then he's off again,

forcing his way out further this time, past the breakers,
until all that can be seen is a bobbing head.

The alarm sounds but a search reveals nothing. On the news
that night it barely rates a mention but three days later

he's spotted in Auckland, sitting outside a café
wearing only a striped towel – sand still in his hair, salt

crystallizing on his skin – quietly sipping coffee,
his hopes of mortality dashed once again.

Photo

There's a photograph of me with my mother – a rare backyard shot,
me perched on the bonnet of the white Escort van,
my mother standing beside me, bare kneed in a homemade dress,
pockets stitched on the front like an apron,
our bodies not quite touching.
All her love is in the gap between us –
in the way she has wiped and stilled her hands,
in the way she's willing to stand and wait
while my brother frames the shot, and in how
she has closed her ears to the sound of the shop's bell
for that brief moment of time. We wait for the camera's click,
hold our smiles against a weak Western District sun.
It's my tenth birthday.
For some reason, I'm wearing flippers.

The Baby-Boomer Teacher Poet Speaks

for Susan Hampton

She says she's still a smoker

though she's given up the habit, says

the lines on her face
are the gift
of thirty years of inhaling.

She says Anne Carson is the most idiosyncratic intelligence
writing in English today.
She says just because there's a funeral it doesn't mean

there was anyone crying.

She says just because they were a parent it doesn't mean they were loved –

says

if you use fear as your method of discipline
people feel only relief
when you die.

She says she does still love him, she thinks,

though she wouldn't call it love.

She says she prefers, now, that things be more ordered –

says the papers and books on the desk look better
when neatly arranged.

She says, let's not worry about my personal shit.

She says she wishes it were the wife not the mistress
sharing the corner at the party with the man in the poem.
She says her days of affairs are over.

She says Ashbery says —

he doesn't understand some of his own poems and feels under no
pressure to do so.
She says just because people are young doesn't mean they are poor.
She says translating other people's documents into understandable
English
pays better than teaching or writing
poetry.

She says you should consider how, and where
you break the line.

Future Tense

You meet her at the door
even though it is not your house. All night,
caught in the wine-warmed banter of old friends and new,
you skirt the edges of each other's conversations, avoid direct talk.
When she approaches, you curb your body language, turn your limbs
away but that same body betrays you – you laugh too loudly
when she laughs – and each time she moves your pulse
quickens, you shift in your seat, tug at your now
too-tight shirt. Outside, a last-quarter moon
has risen above the remnant rainforest
and scant stars pit a sheet-iron sky.
As you say your goodbyes
she is the last one
you kiss. Later,
in the stark familiarity
of the quiet drive home,
she picks a fight with her lover.

Forest Fire

Linton, Victoria. Dec 2, 1998

those who loved them
will never entirely leave
no matter how far they go
their bodies will remember
that burnt sienna day
when the world shifted on its axis
bent forward
and swallowed their men whole

Doorknockers

It was the lack of a front door and an unwillingness
to be rude that started it, the first time.
A nice older lady asking my name, admiring the house,
passing me the pamphlet. To be nice I took it, smiled
as they left, unaware they'd be back so soon –
the second time a pair – the same woman
and a younger man each talking and nodding in turn.
I mumbled thanks, decided to hide upstairs the next time,
keep a lookout for two weeks. They were on to me of course,
left a longer gap; a different time and day so I was stuck out
the back at the washing line when they arrived. She waved
but I stayed put,
keep hanging out clothes, let her struggle up
the rough yard: a necessary cruelness I told myself,
something to give her the hint.
Her smile held as I cut her short, muttering
'You know, it's just not my thing' and stood grinning,
undies in hand. I wanted her to shrug her shoulders
and say, 'Fair enough' and be off, but her face hardened,
she drew in her breath, said, 'There's no doubt the...'
I nodded helplessly, said 'Sorry;' saw too late
what was at stake.
I should have pissed her off in the beginning –
yelled abuse, kicked her in the shins – anything
rather than sabotage her there
in the blazing light of afternoon.

Blood Moon

My daughter drum rolls down the stairs
to announce
a dragon has bitten the moon.

She is eight years old and tonight there is a lunar eclipse.

We wind her and her brother up like tin toys –

send them
spiralling around the room.
At the beach the burnt orange sphere holds them entranced –

they rumble,

digging and rolling like manic pups.

*

The moon is heavy in the spectral sky as we head home,
sand spinning from our hair,
hungry as dragons.

To My Ex-Husband

A guru once told me
real love recognises the other –
and loves them – even when what they want
is not you

Well, that's crap, I thought – and held on
to the bitter end

I'm sorry I wasn't larger of heart, like Phar Lap

Emerald Eye

The woman opposite has an emerald eye – a trick of reflection
from a forest-filled window. Within this room's cathedral light,

we are writing and breathing, snatching at words, scratching
tiny footprints on paper. This water-carved valley is deeper than bone,

as ancient as sound. As the afternoon exhales, we wrestle our history,
confess our obsessions – emblazon our language with stones.

Two Poems, July 2011

Trajectory

for Tim

We are seated, as usual for the last four of your birthdays,
on the east side of the sloping hill
at your grandfather's place, looking northwest
over the paddocks to where the escarpment drops
three hundred feet, across to the ocean
and the lights of Wollongong.

At each of these gatherings we burn a little more
of an ancient eucalypt where it fell years ago, brought down
by termites and the highland wind.
Now its great root mat stands taller than two men.
Its sister towers behind us, its huge limbs
lit orange against the dark sky.

You are showing off on your new red mountain bike,
sliding and stacking on purpose. We are all here: me,
your Dad, your sister, your stepdad, your grandfather
and your friends. At dinner, your stepdad is playing guitar,
and your dad is drinking bourbon and telling us
how the weaner calves this year need cobalt and selenium

because the soil is deficient, and how, when they lack cobalt,
the calves appear to cry, shedding tears from each eye,
and as your dad gets drunker, he muses
on how amazing it is that the three box saplings near the fire
have survived without any protection from the cows
to roughly your own age, and how amazing it is too, that you –

our son – have made it to this: your sixteenth year.
After dinner you and the boys, Lachie, Josh and Ethan
drive off in the rusted ute to your own private camp
by the creek,
complete with tents and gear, campfire, plus
the essentials: laptop, speakers, iPhone.

Your sister Carrie and her friend Tinka are in the shed
perched high on bales of hay – they shoo us away
from their secrets. Later in the night
your dad (drunk) and your stepdad (not quite so drunk)
stagger down the slope on their way to your camp.
I stay by the fire with the dog, and listen

as the sounds of teenage music drifting across
the night paddocks is cut through with your shouts
as they arrive. Above me, the sky is loaded with stars:
to the east the mobile towers of Knights Hill flash out
their aurorae and to the north, airliners blink
their way south. I see a shooting star. It is close to midnight.

The night you were born I was up this late,
and in the boredom of a slow labour, I left the hospital
and walked up the road, leaning against the telegraph poles
at each contraction. I remember it was too cold to stay out
for long, and that the sky that night was full of clouds, not stars.
You took your time – under that swirling sky I did not know

it would take all night and most of the next day for you to arrive.
Tonight, the milky way is crowded, and the planets are lined up
in an arc, and what I want to tell you
is how glad I am that you were born, and how glad I am
to be here, remembering this on the occasion
of your fifteenth birthday,

each of us navigating our own diverging trajectories,
as connected as the stars.

Little Gods

for Carrie

After camping we arrive home weary, smelling of smoke
and highland air – I declare my intention –
to write all afternoon.
But soon the sun, welcome after weeks of biting cold,
draws me to the garden
where I allow my mind to ease and soften
with thoughts of earth and seeds, and of a spring filled
with the kind of abundance only an imagined future
can hold. I pull on boots and gloves, arm myself
with trowel and spade
and set to work, turning over the sodden soil
until my hands blister and my back aches.
My daughter wanders over – barefoot in the damp grass.
She helps for a while, plucking at weeds
in the herb bed. We talk – she has trouble with boys.
I listen, and try hard not to say too much, try to just listen
as I attack the kikuyu runners and self-sown mint
overtaking the bed. Soon she drifts away – I glimpse
her attempts to cajole the pony with mint stems –
he flicks his head and shies – he won't allow her to halter him.
I keep working, and a satisfying rhythm develops, a harmony
of thoughts and actions, a drone in my brain that grounds
me to this moment, this place.
Once the weeds are cleared, I load the barrow with black silt
from the creek bed – a glut of velvet soil
brought down in last month's flood –
and haul
it back to the garden to boost up the beds.

When it's done, I stand and stretch – more satisfied in this
than all else I've achieved this week –
and as I bend to pack up,
five tiny birds arrive – like little gods – a yellow robin,
a red-capped finch, a grey fantail, and two wrens.
The robin is the least shy – perched high
on the climber-bean wire he tilts his head
and looks at me then dips down to snatch up an insect.
The others follow, flitting across the turned soil
in search of grubs. I know the deal – it's the same
with all gods – stay still, keep quiet, wait.
They dart here and there, skittish as young foals, until
as if in response to some universal signal, they fly
away as one, their fragile forms synchronised
as they disappear into the eddying clouds
of the oncoming night's sky river. The July cold
has returned. In the paddock I see my daughter.
She is feeding her pony, her arm around his neck.
His halter is on. I strip off gloves and boots and head inside.
The horse whinnies softly. I have my poem.

Moss

I'm no good at love poems.
Instead, I'll tell you how the wooden box
props open the shed door, how the eaves of the iron roof
bend with the weight of pine needles, how there is dark moss growing
at the base of the chimney and how the unpruned pear strives for the sky
and how – right now – evening mist is sifting through this scene,
dissolving what might-have-been,
if you'd been here.

The Horfield Elegies

Markers by which we find our way back

These are the landmarks I remember –
the church by the weir, the stretch of silver road
by the dairy, peppertrees along the drive.

Arriving I am greeted by the banshee cries of peacocks –
the funereal utterances of dry-country crows,
the clatter-bang of the screen door.

In the kitchen Gwen is drying up the dishes,
Vern is at the table with the paper – one ear out for the hurrahs and shouts
of test cricket emanating from the lounge-room TV.

Out in the backyard, the scent of fallen fruit
from the overburdened orange rises
rotten-sweet in the afternoon air.

Sometimes, it's not just the familiar strata of our childhood
we return to, but the people,
and echoes of lives wholly wedded

to a particular place, which draw us back, to
that sacred, unshakeable terrain
we call home.

Hours, and days — a life re-imagined.

In memory of Ivy Olive Peace

1.

After your funeral
I return to your house
to seek your spiritual grave —
the garden you curated for seventy years.
Sinewy arms hang down from the date palm
planted the year you married, while by the gate
paperbark fingers meet thumbs of oleander above fists
of buffalo grass. Bamboo collarbones criss-cross the porch,
kissing shoulder-blades of jacaranda that fan down the broad back
of the cypress hedge. Next to the shed, stout kurrajong legs
adjoin peppertree hips and around the garden edges
painted pot-plants bunch up like toes.
Along the drive a straight spine
of brittle gums flex
and bend in the heat, whilst
further out, past the reach of the hose,
a drought-wizened pomegranate, encircled
in a ribcage of fishbone ferns, bears —
on one slender, hopeful branch —
a solitary, tough-skinned
fire-red heart.

2.

In the peacock's morning call and the steady drill of cows
down to the milking shed,
I hear the religion of your days, the dedication
you brought to each hour.

This garden bears witness to the chorus around your life
the chatter of finches, the quarrels of wrens,
the paddock shouts of children,
the scrabble of possums on the iron roof.

Your laughter is in the side-step of a copper-tailed skink, your voice
in the glimpse of a half-wild cat – stark against the frost –
and as I move toward the shrouded,
silenced house, the red clay

I walk across conjures up an echo
of your footsteps as it cracks
and breaks
into wafers beneath my feet.

The light we travel at the end of day

On the road past the milking shed
        twilight washes in –
                paints saltbush into coral beds
    blue-green and magenta

Quartz eyes glint in the crackle-glazed road –
        ahead a lone runner
                reaches for the last stretch
    in already aching limbs

Stark flatness all directions bar one:
        to the south
                the rocks of Mount Hope lie cast –
    a beached pod of granite whales

In cooling air, moths draw close,
        scents lift from sun-warmed soil:
                beneath willow trees cows shift weight –
    their hooves tamping salt pans underfoot

and in the shuttering light, the horizon flutters
        like a 1950's girl twirling her favourite dress –
                her face shadowed into plainness
    as darkness falls

Acknowledgements

Several of the poems or versions of them in this collection have previously appeared in:

Australian Poetry Collaboration e zine, Arts Rush, Blue Dog, The Bridport Prize Anthology(UK) 2018, *Cathexis Northwest* (USA) *foame: e, Glint*(USA), *Griffith Review, In A Day It Changes* (PressPress) *Chapbook 2018, Once Wild: Newcastle poetry Prize Anthology 2014, Not Very Quiet Journal, Poetry d'Amour* 2016 and 2018 Anthologies, *Signs: The University of Canberra Vice Chancellors International Poetry Competition anthology* 2018, *Sky Island*(USA), *SquidInk, Stylus Lit, Tangents: Kitchen Table Poets Anthology 2008, The Way To The Well: Central Coast Poets Anthology* 2015, *Wild Honey: Dangerously Poetic Press Byron Writers Prize Anthology* 2011.

My heartfelt thanks go to The Kitchen Table Poets members: Elaine Chin, Irene Wilkie, Colleen Duncan, Chere Le Page, Lyn Kluewer, Jenny Dickerson, Jen Mors and Kate Broadhurst for their critical encouragement, feedback, and friendship over two decades.

I also wish to thank the many poets and mentors whose workshops and feedback have been invaluable to my development as a poet over the years and to the final realisation of this manuscript— in particular: Chris Mansell, David Musgrave, Brook Emery, Nicola Bowery, Harry Laing, Peter Bishop, Les Wicks and the late Deb Westbury.

I am immensely grateful to the following organisations: Australian Society of Authors, The Katherine Susannah Pritchard Writers Centre, Varuna, and the NSW Writers centre for their support in the form of fellowships and mentorships which have been invaluable in the development of this collection.

Finally, thanks to my family and friends, without whom this collection would not have been possible.

www.ingramcontent.com/pod-product-compliance
Lightning Source LLC
Chambersburg PA
CBHW030814090426

42737CB00010B/1266